This book belongs to

Judith Drews

Let's Make a Change

The United Nations' 17 Goals for a Better World

PRESTEL

Munich · London · New York

Join in!

The Planet and the People Need Our Help

All of us – people, plants and animals – need the Earth.
We all live here together, and we have to treat
the planet and each other well.

As you might have heard at school, on the news or from
the adults in your life, the world is facing many problems,
such as war and climate change. People are still mistreating
each other and the planet on which they live.
That needs to change. In order to protect the environment,
we need to act sustainably. We can't consume more resources
than is good for the environment. We have to think of
future generations when we use plants, animals, minerals
and other treasures of the Earth. We also need social
sustainability – that is, we want all people to live a good life.
Social injustices like war, poverty and hunger need to end.

Because there are no easy solutions for these problems,
all of us, no matter how old or young we are, have to be aware
of them and do whatever we can to make a difference.

In 2015, representatives from the 193 member states of
the UN – the United Nations – came together and decided on
17 Sustainable Development Goals to create a better future
for the planet and its people by 2030. To reach these goals,
each and every one of us has to try and make a change!

The 17 Sustainable Development Goals

The 17 Sustainable Development Goals are listed here, and on the following pages you'll find out what they mean and why we need to reach them. We can only succeed if we all help!

❶

No poverty

End poverty in all its forms everywhere.

❷

Zero Hunger

End hunger, achieve food security and improved nutrition, and promote sustainable agriculture.

❸

Good health and well-being

Ensure healthy lives and promote well-being for all at all ages.

❹

Quality education

Ensure inclusive and equitable quality education and promote lifelong learning opportunities for all.

❺

Gender equality

Achieve gender equality and empower all women and girls.

❻

Clean water and sanitation

Ensure availability and sustainable management of water and sanitation for all.

❼

Affordable and clean energy

Ensure access to affordable, reliable, sustainable and modern energy for all.

❽

Decent work and economic growth

Promote sustained, inclusive and sustainable economic growth, full and productive employment and decent work for all.

⑨ Industry, innovation and infrastructure

Build resilient infrastructure, promote inclusive and sustainable
industrialization and foster innovation.

⑩ Reduced inequalities

Reduce inequality within and among countries.

⑪ Sustainable cities and communities

Make cities and human settlements inclusive, safe, resilient and sustainable.

⑫ Responsible consumption and production

Ensure sustainable consumption and production patterns.

⑬ Climate action

Take urgent action to combat climate change and its effects.

⑭ Life below water

Conserve and sustainably use the oceans, seas and marine resources
for sustainable development.

⑮ Life on land

Protect, restore and promote the sustainable use of land ecosystems
by sustainably managing forests, combating desertification, halting and
reversing land degradation and addressing biodiversity loss.

⑯ Peace, justice and strong institutions

Promote peaceful and inclusive societies for sustainable development, provide access to
justice for all and build effective, accountable and inclusive institutions at all levels.

⑰ Partnerships for the goals

Strengthen the means of implementation and revitalize
the Global Partnership for Sustainable Development.

1

We want to end poverty in all its forms everywhere in the world.

While many of us take it for granted to always have food, clothing and a secure home, people living in poverty don't have enough money for these things. Many can't afford to pay for their children's education or for school supplies. In some countries – but not nearly enough countries – there is support for poor people. Their rent is paid by the government and they get a bit of money each month. They can buy what they need in order to survive, but they can't afford to go on holidays or to the cinema. Often, poor people feel socially excluded, and because they tend to be less educated, it is hard for them to overcome poverty. Well-paid jobs often require a high level of education.

We need YOU, because you know what it means to share, and you know there doesn't need to be poverty in the world.

2

We want to end hunger.

Many of us are well off. We live in abundance and our plates are always full. Unfortunately, there are many people in this world who don't have enough to eat and who suffer from hunger. They lack access to good food and important nutrients. Lack of food makes them more vulnerable to diseases. Children, whose physical development is constrained because of poor diet, are especially affected. One cause of hunger is poverty. People who are poor can't afford food. Climate change causes hunger, too, especially when draughts and floods destroy crops.

We need YOU, because you want everyone to have enough food and no one to starve.

3

We want health and well-being for all.

All of us get ill sometimes, but not all sick people receive good care. Some places in the world, especially rural areas, don't have enough medical staff. People there often have to travel far to get help. There are also countries where medical treatments are very expensive. Poor people often can't afford treatment or medicine, so they don't go to the doctor at all, even though they are ill.

We need YOU, because you know everyone should be able to go to the doctor when they are ill.

We want everyone to have access to the best education and training.

Worldwide, there are many children who don't go to school. That's because there are no schools in some places, or because school fees and the cost of school supplies are too high. Children from poor families often go to work early in life to support their families and siblings. In many cases, they can't read or write. Without an education, it is hard to find a well-paid job. Children who were not able to go to school often live in poverty as adults as well.

We need YOU, because you love reading and writing, and you want every child to be able to go to school.

5

We want absolute gender equality.

Everywhere in the world, women and girls are not treated as well as men and boys in different aspects of life. In some countries, for example, girls are not allowed to go to school, and women are often paid less for their work or not at all. Because women often don't have the same access to education and work as men, it is harder for them to be independent.

We need YOU,
because you think
all people in this world
are equally important.

6

We want clean water and proper sanitation to be available for everyone.

Many of us take water for granted. We turn on the tap and it flows. But there are many people who don't have access to clean water. They not only lack drinking water, they also lack sanitary facilities like toilets, sinks and showers. Where there are no toilets, diseases and bacteria spread more easily.

We need YOU, because you know how important water, and especially drinking water, is for us.

7

We want everyone to be able to afford renewable and sustainable energy.

No matter if we use it for the batteries in our phones, for cooking at home, for the computers at school or at work, for medical devices in hospitals, or for machines in big factories – most of us need electricity in our daily lives. But there are still areas in the world where people have to live without electricity. In many places, moreover, the way people get their energy is bad for them and for the environment. The majority of people lack access to clean sources of energy like hydroelectric power and wind energy.

We need YOU, because together we can provide better power on Earth without harming nature.

8

We want dignified work and employment for all.

Many people are poor, even though they work very hard. In the textile industry, for example, people, especially women, work for more than twelve hours a day in stuffy rooms with hardly any breaks. Women who produce T-shirts and jeans are exposed to poisonous chemicals harming their health, and they earn so little money that they can barely survive. Poor people who work in other industries, like agriculture, often labor under unfair conditions as well.

We need YOU, because you want everyone to have good work and be able to support themselves and their families.

9

We want new ideas to improve our living conditions and preserve the environment.

In our daily lives, we often have to travel long distances. We journey from home to school, to the playground or to the doctor's office. In big cities, these places can be far away from each other, while rural areas sometimes lack them altogether. It's important that schools, hospitals and other public places are easy to reach for everyone, even when they don't have a car. To achieve this goal, we need public transportation that all can use. We also need new inventions that help improve everyone's lives – but without harming people or the environment.

We need you, because you are interested in technology, and your mind is filled with great ideas.

We want less disparity because we are all equally important.

The country in which you are born has a big impact on the opportunities you're going to have in life. There are poor countries and rich countries. In most rich countries, all children can go to school and people can receive health care. Poor countries, however, often lack these benefits. Even within an individual country, there can be big differences in opportunities for different people. Some families have enough money to go on vacation every summer or to enroll their children in sports clubs, while others can't afford these things.

We need YOU, because you understand that it's wrong when some people have a lot and others very little.

11

We want to prepare our homes for climate change with sustainable ideas.

People in cities live in very different ways. Some live in big houses by themselves or with a few others, while many large families often have to share tiny apartments together. Still others don't have a home at all and must survive on the street. Cities also have other problems. Where there are lots of people, there will be lots of waste, and the many cars in big cities pollute the air. In addition, though many cities are built in a way that makes it easy to access places on foot, this access can be limited for people in a wheelchair or with a stroller.

We need YOU, because you know we need to build cities in a way that doesn't harm nature and enables everyone to live well.

① ②

We want our resources to be used sustainably and our goods to be produced in an environmentally conscious way.

We are used to supermarkets and other stores always having what we need or want. Some people always want to have the latest fashion or the newest technology. In order to produce all these things, energy and lots of resources are being spent. It also generates a lot of waste when we always buy something new, even though our old things still work.

We need YOU, because you carefully think about what you really need, and don't throw away things that could still be used.

1 3

We urgently need good ideas for more climate action.

Because our CO_2-emissions are too high, the climate on Earth is changing. This problem affects all people in the world. Some areas get so hot due to climate change that they suffer many draughts and forest fires. Other places get floods, landslides and heavy storms, which destroy crops, people's homes, and habitats for animals and plants.

We need YOU, because you know we need to protect our climate so we can live on Earth for a very long time.

We want to protect life in our oceans.

The seas make up more than two-thirds of the Earth, and they are home to numerous animals and plants. Unfortunately, a lot of waste ends up in the sea and harms marine life. Plastic is not biodegradable, and it breaks down into smaller and smaller pieces that get eaten by fish. Plastic also ends up in our bellies when we eat fish. In addition, way too many fish are caught at once in big nets, endangering the survival of many types of fish. Sometimes, other animals get tangled in the nets and die as well.

We need YOU, because you love the oceans on our blue planet and want to protect them.

15

We want to improve life on land for everyone.

The habitats of plants and animals on land are threatened. Because more and more people are moving to cities, more houses are being built and the cities are expanding. This growth means that many forests and meadows are disappearing. Other forests are being cleared to make space for fields, on which food for livestock is grown. A lot of animals are losing their habitat and many plants are becoming endangered. In addition, because of climate change, more and more areas are drying up and becoming uninhabitable deserts.

We need YOU, because you have known the importance of animals and plants for a long time.

16

We want peace, justice and equitable legal systems.

In some countries of the world, there is war. Many people have to flee their homes and communities to live safely. There are also countries where people can't speak their opinions freely, and where they have no access to fair courts of law.

We need YOU, because you think that everyone should live in freedom and without fear of war and violence.

17

We want worldwide partnerships to reach these goals together.

The 17 Sustainable Development Goals are meant to create a better world for all people. That's why all of us have to work together to achieve them. We have to treat each other with respect and listen to one another. That way, we can recognize problems and solve them together.

We need YOU, because we want to save the Earth together.

Now!

Let's Make A Change!
What can you do?

Try not to waste food. Only put on your plate what you are going to eat.

✳

Be mindful with water. Don't leave the tap running while you brush your teeth.

✳

Save electricity when you can. It can be as simple as turning off the lights
when you leave the room or not keeping your phone plugged in all night long.

✳

Think carefully about what you have and what you need before
you buy new things.

✳

Donate clothes, toys and school supplies you no longer need.

✳

Walk, cycle or use public transportation whenever possible.

✳

Avoid plastic when you can. You could take a tote bag with you
when you go shopping, and bring a reusable water bottle.

✳

Be respectful of the nature around you. Don't litter in or damage nature reserves.

✳

Be creative and curious. Draw pictures or write down your ideas
and inventions for a better world.

✳

Help others when you can. If there's something you're really good
at doing and someone else is struggling with it, try to help them out.

✳

Have open conversations about gender and equality.

✳

Be kind and respectful to the people around you.

✳

Tell your friends and family about the goals and
encourage them to make a change.

Thanks for your ideas for this book:
Karl, Lucie, Luise, Paul and Robert

© for the German edition: 2023 Verlagshaus Jacoby & Stuart GmbH, Berlin, Germany
© for the English edition: 2024, Prestel Verlag, Munich · London · New York
A member of Penguin Random House Verlagsgruppe GmbH
Neumarkter Strasse 28 · 81673 Munich
© illustrations: Judith Drews
© text: Judith Drews and Fatima Grieser

Library of Congress Control Number: 2023921026
A CIP catalogue record for this book is available from the British Library.

Translated from the German by Fatima Grieser
Editorial direction: Doris Kutschbach
Copyediting: Brad Finger
Production management and typesetting: Susanne Hermann
Printing and binding: TBB, a.s., Banská Bystrica

MIX
Paper | Supporting responsible forestry
FSC® C022120
FSC www.fsc.org

Penguin Random House Verlagsgruppe FSC® N001967

Printed in Slovakia
ISBN 978-3-7913-7560-1
www.prestel.com